# SPIES

## WARNING: WWII SECRET AGENTS INSIDE

Terry Deary
Illustrated by Mike Phillips

**SCHOLASTIC**

To Alyx Price for her dedication. TD

Scholastic Children's Books,
Euston House, 24 Eversholt Street,
London, NW1 1DB, UK

A division of Scholastic Ltd
London ~ New York ~ Toronto ~ Sydney ~ Auckland
Mexico City ~ New Delhi ~ Hong Kong

Editorial Director: Lisa Edwards
Editors: Victoria Garrard, Stefanie Smith and Catriona Clarke

First published in the UK by Scholastic Ltd, 2009

Text copyright © Terry Deary, 2009
Cover illustration copyright © Martin Brown, 2009
Inside illustrations by Mike Phillips, based on the style of the
original *Horrible Histories* artwork by Martin Brown
Illustrations copyright © Mike Phillips, 2009
Colour by Geri Ford
All rights reserved

ISBN 978 1407 10567 3

Printed and bound by Tien Wah Press Pte. Ltd, Malaysia

2 4 6 8 10 9 7 5 3 1

The right of Terry Deary, Martin Brown and Mike Phillips to be identified as the author and
illustrators of this work respectively has been asserted by them in accordance with the Copyright,
Designs and Patents Act, 1988.

# CONTENTS

INTRODUCTION 5
TERRIBLE TIMELINE 7
SUPER SPIES 9
DISGUISES 18
CRACKING CODES 24
GREAT GADGETS 29
TOP TIPS 34
RUTHLESS RESISTANCE 40
SAVAGE SABOTAGE 46
TORTURE OF THE TEST 51
BOOBY TRAPS 55
CLEVER CAMOUFLAGE 60
FOUL FACTS 65
BLASTING BOMBS 70
DEAD WRONG 73
SOE SCIENCE SECRETS 78
TORTURE AND TERROR 81
SPY ENDS 86
EPILOGUE 91

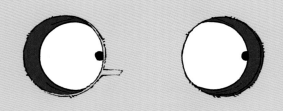

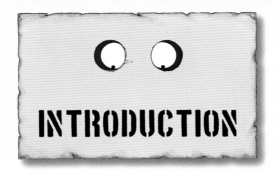

# INTRODUCTION

## BEWARE THE CAMEL POO.

There you are. You are walking across a desert in North Africa. The sun is setting and it is cooler. You are enjoying your walk.

You are a spy, of course. I mean to say, you wouldn't be in a desert for a holiday. You are following enemy tank tracks across the desert. When you find the enemy base you can report back. Your air force can find them and wipe them out.

And then you see it! In the middle of the desert track. A big brown lump of camel poo!

It is dotted across the track like … like camel poo. What do you do?

Kick it out of the way?
Maybe not.

Jump on it and flatten it?
Maybe not.

Look for camel footprints in the sand. Can you see any? No, you can only see tank tracks.

If you are a top spy you will see the truth at once. It's a trap. There are no camels and those brown blobs aren't camel poo. They are bombs (mines) that are made to look like camel droppings.

If you kick one or stand on one it will blow a leg off your body … if you are lucky. If you are unlucky it will blow your body off your leg.

You are in the deadly world of spies where nothing is what it seems – not even camel poo. Where death is just around the corner.

You may think the camel story is a joke. But it's NOT. In the Second World War, spies really DID drop mines disguised as dung. It's not a story – it's history. It's not the sort of history you learn in school. It is Horrible History.

And it is Horrible History that will keep you alive in the world of spies – or 'espionage' if you want the posh word.

Here is a book of all the terrible tricks to look out for. A handbook for Second World War spies.

Read it and you may just survive. Even better, read it, learn it, then eat it.

This book comes in special, secret flavours – flavours like rat poison, snot-flavour ice cream, history-teacher-sock-scented crisps and, of course, camel dung.

Enjoy.

# TERRIBLE TIMELINE

**SEPTEMBER 1939** Britain and her friends (France, Canada, Australia, New Zealand) go to war with Germany and her friends (Austria, Italy, Japan). The Second World War has begun.

**JUNE 1940** The Nazi German army enters Paris. France is defeated. But the 'Free French' want to fight on ... with the help of Brit secret agents.

ALL THIS INVENTING'S GONE TO HIS HEAD!

**JULY 1940** Britain forms the Special Operations Executive – the SOE – to make secret war on its enemies. They will train spies and invent secret weapons.

**SEPTEMBER 1940** Nazi leader Adolf Hitler is planning Operation Sea Lion – the invasion of Britain. He needs German spies in Britain to help the plans.

**JUNE 1941** Germany turns and attacks old friend Russia. B-i-g mistake. Russia will now fight with the Brits.

**DECEMBER 1941** The Japanese bomb a US base at Pearl Harbor in the Pacific Ocean. Next day the US joins the war with Britain. B-i-g help.

**27 MAY 1942** Czech freedom fighters assassinate top Nazi Reinhard Heydrich. They were trained by the Brits. It was the only British assassination plot that worked.

**JUNE 1942** The US has its own spies, called the Office of Strategic Services or OSS.

**8 NOVEMBER 1842** Operation Torch begins – the US and British armies attack the Germans in North Africa.

**FEBRUARY 1943** German freedom fighters hate Hitler's Nazis. They form a secret group called the 'White Rose' in Germany. They're betrayed. The Nazis execute them.

**JULY 1943** 25,000 German troops have had itching powder added to their clothes by spies who are really up to scratch.

**OCTOBER 1943** Italy surrenders and joins Britain in the fight against Germany.

**FEBRUARY 1944** French freedom fighters call for a 'Rat Week' … they plan to kill as many German secret police (Gestapo) as they can. No mean feat. At least 12 Gestapo officers are assassinated.

I'M NOT TICKLED PINK ABOUT THIS!

**JUNE 1944** Spies in Denmark report German sheds full of dead rats. They believe the plan is to drop them on Britain and spread the Black Death. (It never happened.) Brit, Canadian and US troops land in France on 'D-Day' and march towards Germany.

**19 AUGUST 1944** The French freedom fighters (the Resistance) start fighting against the Germans in Paris – not a secret army any longer.

**8 MAY 1945** Germany surrenders to Russian, British and American forces. Japan fights on until August.

**15 JANUARY 1946** The British spy group, the SOE, closes down. But spying won't stop.

# SUPER SPIES

In the Second World War there were all sorts of spies. Some were mad for the money – some were the bravest people in history. Which would you be?

**Garbo (Juan Pujol) 1912–1988**

Juan Pujol in Lisbon wanted to be a spy for the British but the British weren't sure. So he offered to spy for Germany. The Germans said, 'Ja!'

Pujol read books and newspapers and sent reports to Germany about life in Britain. In fact he never left Lisbon.

And THEN the Brits said he could work for them!

Greta Garbo was a famous actress. The Brits said Pujol was such a good actor that should be his code name.

The Brits called Pujol 'Garbo' and gave him lots of lies to pass on to the Germans. The Germans thought he was so wonderful they said...

Garbo invented 27 spies who (he said) were working for him. The Germans paid them too!

In June 1944 Garbo told the Germans what they were desperate to hear: all about the Brit plans to invade France (D-Day).

Where were the Brit and US forces going to land?

Of course the invasion force landed in Normandy. Germany was defeated.

## Zigzag (Eddie Chapman) 1914–1997

Eddie Chapman was a crook. On the island of Jersey he was caught robbing a dance-hall safe and sent to prison for 15 years.

But the Germans invaded Jersey and offered him a job. 'Go back to England. Spy for Germany!'

Eddie dropped into England ... and told the Brit spy chiefs just what had happened. They told him to carry on spying for Germany – but the Brits would tell him what to say.

In 1944 the Germans sent him a message...

WE ARE FIRING ROCKET BOMBS ON LONDON. TELL US IF WE ARE HITTING THE TARGET!

The bombs WERE hitting the heart of London and thousands of people were dying. So Eddie was told to send a crafty message...

THE BOMBS ARE SHOOTING *OVER* LONDON. YOU NEED TO DROP THEM SHORTER!

And that's just what the Germans did. The rockets started to fall harmlessly in fields south of London.

GOOD CHAP, CHAPMAN

### ☠ DID YOU KNOW...? ☠

In 1966 a film was made about Eddie Chapman's life as a crook and a spy. It is called *Triple Cross*.
Eddie didn't think much of the film!

## Louise (Violette Szabo) 1921–1945

Violette was just 20 when she met a French soldier, Etienne Szabo, and married him in London.

Etienne went off to fight against Germany and was killed. Violette wanted revenge. She left her baby daughter and trained to fight with the Resistance in France.

Her first job was dangerous…

Violette did a great job even though she was arrested twice. She flew back to London.

Her second trip didn't have such a happy ending.

On 10 June 1944 she was with the Resistance leader when they ran into a troop of German soldiers…

SHE WAS TAKEN AND TORTURED...

NOOOOOOOO!

VIOLETTE WAS TAKEN TO RAVENSBRÜCK CAMP AND SET TO DO HARD LABOUR. IN FEBRUARY, SHE WAS EXECUTED

☠ **DID YOU KNOW…?** ☠

A film was made about Violette's life and work. It is called *Carve Her Name with Pride*.

## Wilhelm Lonkowski (b. 1893)

This nasty Nazi worked in America before the war started.

I SET UP A SPY RING IN NEW YORK AND THEY COLLECTED SECRETS ABOUT AEROPLANES

Then he had to find a way to get the secrets back to Germany.

I DECIDED TO SEND THEM BY SHIP. A SHIP CALLED EUROPA WAS GOING FROM NEW YORK TO GERMANY AND ONE OF THE SERVANTS ON BOARD WAS A NAZI

Now Lonkowski couldn't just hand over a bunch of secret papers, could he?

I HID THEM IN A VIOLIN CASE AND MET THE SERVANT FROM THE EUROPA AT THE DOCKS. THAT'S WHEN SOMETHING WENT WRONG!

A US customs officer saw the case ... and his hobby was violins! He asked to see the violin. The ship's servant made a run for it but...

I WAS ARRESTED WHEN HE FOUND THE PAPERS

They questioned Lonkowski all night but decided not to hold him. The American spy-catchers made some stupid mistakes ... so stupid even YOU wouldn't make them!

THEY DIDN'T ASK MY NAME, THEY DIDN'T ASK MY ADDRESS ... AND THEY TOLD ME TO COME BACK TO THE POLICE STATION IN THREE DAYS' TIME!

Of course Lonkowski did NOT go back in three days' time – would YOU? He headed for Canada then escaped to Germany.

WHEN I GOT HOME I WAS TREATED LIKE A HERO AND MASTER SPY! SHAME I HAD TO LEAVE THE VIOLIN!

## ☣ Dɪᴅ ʏᴏᴜ ᴋɴᴏᴡ…? ☣

Not all German spies in America became heroes. Karl Franz Rekowski had the code name 'Rex' … well, it's easier to spell. There were a lot of Irish rebels in the USA at the time and Rex had a great idea…

I WILL PAY THE IRISH TO SABOTAGE THE AMERICAN FACTORIES

It all went really well. Rex handed over the money…

SURE IT'S A BARGAIN YOU'RE GETTING THERE, REX, ME OLD FRIEND!

… then the Irish gave him reports on how their plots were going…

SEE THAT SHADOW ON THE MOON? THAT'S THE FACTORY WE BLEW UP LAST WEEK. BLEW IT ALL THE WAY TO THE MOON, SO WE DID!

AMAZING! I'LL TELL BERLIN!

AND GIVE US MORE MONEY

When the Irish read that there was going to be a public meeting to talk about the war, they went to Rex with an odd request…

WE COULD WRECK THE MEETING WITH BOMBS!

KILL THOUSANDS?

STINK BOMBS!

Rex sent an order back to Berlin … for stink bombs.

ZEY ARE HAVING ZE LAUGH!

It took a while for Rex to discover the truth. The Irish were taking the money but doing nothing – they just made up stories about the sabotage plots.

**Nancy Wake (1912–)**

Nancy Wake was an Australian who helped the French Resistance in Marseilles at the start of the war. She escaped to England, but had to leave her husband behind. Nancy trained with the SOE and returned to France to help the Resistance at Auvergne.

Nancy got a shock when the Resistance leader Gaspart said…

When Nancy argued they said they'd shoot her. Just in time a radio operator, Denis Rake, landed and showed how useful the SOE could be.

Nancy sent radio messages for more weapons. She cycled from Resistance group to Resistance group, taking orders and having guns dropped.

A massive German force of 22,000 troops was sent to crush them. Nancy drove across the battlefield, delivering bullets and carrying the wounded to safety.

In the gun battle Denis Rake's radio was wrecked. Nancy set off on her bike to find the nearest SOE radio. There was not enough petrol for such a long journey and the tracks were too narrow and rocky to go by car.

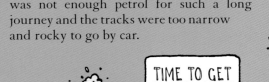

She cycled for 36 hours to send a signal to Britain. Then she cycled straight back to the battlefield – another 36 hours. She was tired and bleeding, but she saved the Resistance. They won the battle.

After the war she went back to Marseilles to find her husband. She was told…

# DISGUISES

**W**ant to fool the enemy? Change the way you look. The SOE invented creams like Mepacreme that made a spy with pale skin turn yellow then dark brown. Carotene (made from carrot juice) turned you orange-brown. 'Wrinkle Cream' made you look old and sick.

> MAKES YOU LOOK OLD AND SICK? SO DOES TEACHING HISTORY TO CLASS 4D ON A FRIDAY AFTERNOON!

Here are a few other tips if you want to be a master spy…

### Fake feet
British spies landing on Japanese islands during the Second World War had a problem with beach landings. They would leave prints of their boots in the sand as they walked up the beach from their landing boats. The SOE came up with an answer. They made rubber prints of bare feet that strapped onto sandals and left footprints in the sand. Anyone seeing them would guess it was just a native … maybe.

There were just two things wrong with this amazing disguise:

**1.** It would have been easier for agents to just take their boots off and walk barefoot up the beach and

**2.** A Japanese defender, seeing the footprints, may just have suspected they belonged to a British agent walking barefoot up the beach!

**Was it worth it?**
Other sandals had the print of a Japanese army boot on the sole. A much better idea to confuse the enemy. Maybe...

## Funny faces
Most people think of false beards and wigs as quick disguises for spies. Real spies know how difficult it is to make a false beard look natural. It is easier for them to shave off hair rather than try to add it.

Cheek pads inside the mouth could change the shape of the face and some spies had surgery to alter their appearance.

A Danish agent had his big nose chopped short and no one knew him when he went back to Denmark to spy.

Sir James Hutchison wanted to drop into France in 1944 but was sure the Germans would know his famous face. He had the doctors change it. He then said…

*Even my own daughter didn't know me!*

But his friends said he still looked the same!

## Secret snaps

Spies who wanted to take pictures of foreign buildings often pretended to be on holiday. They stood a friend in front of their camera but were really taking a picture of the building behind their friend. (Because the person in the picture was often someone's relative, these pictures became known as 'Aunt Minnies'.)

One British spy was cycling alone in Austria before the Second World War. He made friends with the guards at a secret army camp. He asked the guards if he could have their pictures to take home and they posed for him while he took photographs of the defences behind them!

## Poo hoo

Are you a British spy working in Germany? Need to get a few days off?

> I DON'T WANT TO BE IN THE FACTORY WHEN OUR BOMBS GO OFF!

Then go to the doctor and show him a bit of your poo. If it is bloodstained he will say you are sick.

How do you get bloodstained poo? Swallow dried blood.

> I THINK I'LL TAKE MY CHANCE WITH THE BOMB!

## Perfect pants

If the Nazis caught you spying in France they would look at your clothes. If they were made in Britain you were in d-e-e-p trouble.

So the SOE made clothes in French styles with French labels.

Your suit, socks, ties and shoes were all made to look French. Men carried French razors and spies had French pens and pencils.

Even your knickers had French labels in them.

## Neat Nazis

The SOE could even give you a fake German army uniform. Not many spies used these – if they needed one when they arrived in France then they simply nicked one.

> IT HELPS IF YOU'RE NOT TOO PICKY!

## Hair horror

Dying your hair causes problems when your hair starts to grow back. You need to keep dying it – not easy if you are hiding from the enemy.

French agent Pierre Brossolette dyed his hair black and fooled the Germans when he was captured. But when he was held in prison for a while his red hair began to grow through. He was then tortured to tell the truth.

Pierre killed himself by jumping from a window.

FIRST HE DYED...

AND THEN HE DIED!

## Complete kit

Spies in France could carry lots of useful things hidden in their luggage. If they were stopped they would look like a simple traveller. Can you find where the secrets are hidden?

Get six out of six and you live! Any less and you will be executed ... probably.

1. A TUBE OF TOOTHPASTE HIDES...

2. A TIE HIDES...

3. A DOOR KEY HIDES...

4. A BAR OF SOAP HIDES...

5. A HAIRBRUSH HIDES...

6. A POCKET CHESS SET HIDES...

A. A MINIATURE FILM

B. MONEY

C. A RUBBER BALLOON WITH A MESSAGE

D. MAPS

E. A SECRET CODE PRINTED ON SILK

F. A MESSAGE PRINTED ON SILK

**Answers:**

1. A tube of toothpaste hides (C) a rubber balloon with a message.

2. A tie hides (E) a secret code printed on silk.

3. A door key hides (A) a miniature film.

4. A bar of soap hides (F) a message printed on silk.

5. A hairbrush hides (B) money.

6. A pocket chess set hides (D) maps.

# CRACKING CODES

A spy can't use the phone. It's too easy for the enemy to listen. Anyway, in a war, the phone lines are often wrecked.

So a spy sends messages by radio. Again the enemy can listen. So what you have to do is use a secret code.

The Germans used a machine called Enigma to turn their messages into a jumble. Another Enigma machine would receive the jumbled message and turn it back into sense.

What the Germans never knew was that the Brits had their own Enigma machines. Many 'secret' German messages weren't secret at all.

## Apron to Yoke

A French woman was able to send messages to spies across the valley from her house, using her washing line.

She hung out garments that spelled out the message. Her alphabet used the English language to confuse the Germans even further. It read as follows:

**Apron, Blouse, Collar, Duster, Eiderdown, Frock, Gloves, Handkerchief, Jacket, Knickers, Lace, Mat, Night-dress, Overall, Pants, Quilt, Roller-towel, Skirt, Trousers, Undershirt, Vest, Waistcoat, Yoke.**

## Navaho know-how

The Americans had a clever way of keeping their messages secret from their Japanese enemies.

They employed Native American Indians of the Navaho tribe to send messages in their language.

There were only about 30 people in the world who spoke Navaho … and none of them were Japanese.

Here are some of their words…

a-chin – nose
a-kha lin – oil
bi-so-dih – pig
chindi – devil
d-ah – tea

dibeh – sheep
lha-cha-eh – dog
shi-da – uncle
tkin – ice

Here's how it worked:
A message was sent in Navaho…

The man who heard the message turned it into English…

CHA DZEH AH-JAD NASH-DOIE-TSO NE-AHS-JAH

HAT ELK LEG LION OWL

Take the first letter of each English word and you have the message! (No I am NOT going to tell you what this message says – do it yourself, dibeh d-ah shi-da bi-so-dih tkin chindi.)

(If you want to call your history teacher 'dibeh d-ah shi-da bi-so-dih tkin chindi' then don't let me stop you. Just make sure he doesn't know Navaho!)

OH, SO I'M STUPID, AM I?

AH! ER ... A-CHIN A-KHALIN!

## Old code

You can still use some wartime tips to send your own secret messages.

The Greek writer Polybius (203–120 BC) came up with the number square. The letters of the alphabet were arranged into five rows of five columns.

|   | 1 | 2 | 3 | 4 | 5 |
|---|---|---|---|---|---|
| 1 | G | Q | B | T | O |
| 2 | D | N | L | X | J |
| 3 | R | A | W | F | Y/Z |
| 4 | E | V | P | S | I |
| 5 | K | U | M | C | H |

So 'A' is 2 across and 3 down, or 23. 'B' is 31 and 'D' is 12. So 31-23-12 spells 'BAD'.

Amazingly this type of code was still being used by the French Resistance in the Second World War, 2000 years later.

33 51 25 32 12 – 53 51 25 – 31 14 32 54 14 24 14 – 54 41 ?

22 51 22!

## Card trick
Here's a simple spy trick you can try.

• Take a pack of cards and arrange them some way you can remember ... maybe aces, twos, threes and so on, with the clubs first, spades second, diamonds third and hearts last.
• Write a message on the side of the pack.
• Shuffle the pack.
• The message disappears till the cards are put back (by your spy friend) into the right order.

## Book bafflers
Take a book – any book except this one – and a pin.

Prick a hole in one letter on each page to spell out your message.

The message can only be read when the pages are held up to a light.

What if your spy mate is in another country? Just make sure you each have a copy of the same book. Then send your mate the page, line, word and letter that you want.

So 27-15-4-2 means...

> TURN TO PAGE 27, LOOK AT THE FIFTEENTH LINE AND THE FOURTH WORD. THE LETTER YOU WANT IS THE SECOND LETTER OF THE WORD

Of course you do NOT tell anyone else the name of the book.

## Sneaky second

A German spy sent a letter from America to tell his spy masters when the US warship Pershing would sail from New York. German submarines could be waiting for it. He wrote…

> Apparently neutral's protest is thoroughly discounted and ignored. Isman hard hit. Blockade issue affects pretext for embargo on by-products, ejecting suets and vegetable oils.

Uh? Take the second letter of each word to spell out the message.

## Nazi niftiness

The Nazis simply invented their own alphabet. Fine … until an enemy spy gets a copy, then it's a waste of time.

# GREAT GADGETS

Spies often need the help of clever tricks and gadgets. Some in the Second World War were wonderful, and some just plain weird.

## 1 Marvellous mikes

An American spy went to Paris and took a room near the German air force headquarters.

He set up a powerful microphone so he could listen to everything in the German building. The caretaker told the Germans the spy was his cousin.

Then the spy said…

He then spent the next year listening to the enemy.

## 2 Powerful prunes

Doreen Mulot was an SOE agent in London. One of her jobs was to help British prisoners in Germany to escape. Doreen described how her SOE friends used prunes – dried and shrunken plums – to help escapees.

WE FILLED A BATH WITH WATER THEN DROPPED IN A BOX OF PRUNES

SPLOSH!

THE WATER MADE THE PRUNES GO SOFT AND SWELL UP. WE PICKED OUT THE STONES

WE SLIPPED ESCAPE MATERIALS INSIDE THE PRUNES

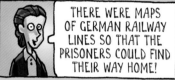

THERE WERE MAPS OF GERMAN RAILWAY LINES SO THAT THE PRISONERS COULD FIND THEIR WAY HOME!

The prunes were then sent as gifts to the prisons and the German guards passed them on to the prisoners.

Doreen also sent diaries, recipe books and dictionaries. At least, that's what they looked like. In fact they were books telling you how to sabotage German roads, trains and factories.

GREAT! NOW ALL WE NEED TO DO IS ESCAPE!

CHOKE!

## 3 Perfect parachutes

Agents usually dropped into France on parachutes.

At first they used parachutes called 'A' parachutes, but these caused a lot of accidents. Splat!

They switched to 'X' parachutes, which were packed in a different way and were safer.

They also wore special suits for jumping. These were called 'striptease suits' because they could be ripped off quickly.

These suits...

WERE WARM AND WINDPROOF

HAD A POCKET FOR A KNIFE (TO CUT ROPES IF THE PARACHUTE GOT CAUGHT IN A TREE)

WERE PRINTED WITH A GREEN AND BROWN PATTERN FOR CAMOUFLAGE

HAD A SPECIAL PAD TO SAVE YOU HURTING YOUR BUM WHEN YOU LANDED

HAD A PISTOL (TO FIGHT IF THE GERMANS WERE WAITING FOR YOU)

CONTAINED FOOD SUPPLIES (WHILE YOU WAITED FOR FRIENDS TO FIND YOU)

HAD A POCKET FOR A KNIFE (TO CUT ROPES IF THE PARACHUTE GOT CAUGHT IN A TREE)

Of course if the parachute failed to open, the spade would come in extra handy … you could dig a grave and bury yourself!

## 🕱 DID YOU KNOW…? 🕱

The SOE invented a special floating suit for agents dropped into water. A Dutch agent tried it. The suit worked.

But an SOE spy in Norway wore one to try to swim to German ships in the harbour. He was going to plant magnetic bombs (mines) on the ships. He stepped into the water…

… and sank to the bottom like a brick.

He managed to climb out. The suit was full of water. The bomb had been tucked inside the suit and had given him a puncture.

## 4 Terror torches

A hand grenade is a small bomb you can throw at an enemy. It explodes five seconds after you let it go (so you don't kill yourself … unless you drop it at your feet).

How could a spy carry a hand grenade and not be caught if he was searched?

The SOE made grenades that looked like torches. Flashlights became flash-bangs.

## 5 Cycle power

SOE radios could be very heavy – some weighed 20 kilos. And they used a lot of battery power. Some agents were given a special bicycle. As they pedalled they made electricity to power the radio.

One agent reported…

## 6 Poison prick

If you can get close enough to your enemy then you might like to jab him with a syringe full of poison.

Agents who set out to assassinate Nazi nasty Reinhard Heydrich carried a syringe of poison.

Just to be sure, they also carried three guns, 200 bullets and ten bombs!

They didn't need the poison.

## 7 Pen pain

If you are captured then you could escape by blinding your enemy for a couple of minutes. Tear gas makes eyes water and sting. The SOE came up with a pen that sent out a jet of tear gas.

They could be very handy in your history exams as you cry over the test paper!

## 8 Baffling bloodhounds

If the enemy thinks you have landed in their area they may set dogs to sniff you out.

The answer is to drag something smelly behind you for a mile or two. The smell will hide your smell and you can escape.

The smelly stuff might be aniseed. The SOE gave spies a bag on a rope. All they had to do was pop the bag with a pin to let out the smell.

Poor pooches wouldn't know which way to turn.

## 9 Can bang

The SOE invented exploding oilcans. Leave them around for a German mechanic to find.

Not only will he blow himself up but he'll damage the car or tank he's working on and maybe the garage too.

## 10 Savage soap

A bar of soap could be left in an enemy camp. It works well for a few days. Then, when the soap wears down, water gets in and sets a fierce flare off. The enemy burns his hands and face.

(If he is in the bath at the time you can imagine what else he'll sizzle.)

A shaving brush can be packed with the flare material. Again, as soon as it is left in water, it bursts into flame. That's what you call a close shave.

# TOP TIPS

Here are some real tricks tried by spies in the Second World War. But careful ... they don't all work!

**Invisible stink**

Invisible ink has been used for thousands of years and has been made from milk, vinegar, lemon juice and even urine!

If you ever get a letter smelling like a toilet it is probably from a spy.

Sometimes invisible maps were drawn on a plain white handkerchief. All you had to do was piddle on the handkerchief and the hidden map appeared. (Then remember not to blow your nose.)

---

**❈ DID YOU KNOW…? ❈**

You can make your own invisible ink simply – and cleanly – using any of these…

**onion juice • vinegar • apple juice • lemon juice**

Carefully heat the writing in front of a candle to make the message appear.

Or use milk and rub in ashes or dust to see the message. The Nazis used milky messages.

---

## Drop dead

Spies who want to pass on messages need a 'letter-box' – not a hole in somebody's door but simply a safe place to leave a message for a partner to collect.

A 'live letter-box' is a person who will hold the message for you and a 'dead letter-box' (or 'dead drop') is just an agreed place.

A dead letter-box can be a hollow tree, a hole in the ground or the boot of a parked car. Anywhere that a message can be hidden in fact.

Some Brit spies used a hollow cross on a grave in a churchyard for messages.

## Secret smoke

## Factory fire

The Germans used prisoners as slave labour in factories. The slaves hated the German masters.

The SOE idea was to give firebombs to German slave workers. The workers could use them to start fires.

This idea was never tried.

## Dead clever

The most gruesome Dutch messenger was a corpse. The message was hidden under the body in a coffin so it could be smuggled across the border. The German border guard did not want to search the corpse. The enemy soldiers even gave it a guard of honour as it took its secrets through their checkpoint.

## Para power

Spies were dropped into enemy countries by parachute and then had to bury the parachutes. But the German air force sometimes dropped empty parachutes on Britain to make the British think there were spies everywhere and waste police and Home Guard time in looking for them.

## Cunning corpse

Before the British landed in Italy they 'accidentally' lost a 'secret' message that showed plans to attack through Greece and Sardinia. (The truth is they meant to go through Sicily).

The secret message was planted on a dead body and dropped into the Mediterranean Sea for the Germans to find. The corpse was given fake papers. They showed he was 'Major Martin'. His pockets held bills, theatre tickets and love letters – all faked – as well as the secret plans for the phoney Greece attack.

The Germans fell for the trick and rushed to defend Greece while their enemies landed in Sicily.

The real name of the dead man is still a secret – he is simply known as 'The Man Who Never Was'.
But Horrible Histories can tell you…

- 'The Man Who Never Was' was a poor tramp from Wales called Glyndwr Michael.
- When the war started he moved to London to make money by begging.
- When he failed he took rat-poison and died.
- The body snatchers of the SOE turned him into Major Martin.

Glyndwr went from zero to hero with a dose of rat poison.

## 🦇 DID YOU KNOW…? 🦇

There were lots of people who 'never were'.

- German leader Adolf Hitler had up to six men who looked like him so his enemies never knew where he really was. But at the end of the war the Germans had an even better idea! Let Hitler escape. Tell the enemies, 'Hitler is dead! And here is the body to prove it!' Where did they find a body? They shot one of the men who looked like Hitler. Because of this trick people believed Hitler was alive long after the war. (I think he taught me maths when I was 11 years old.) Were they right?

- Brit General Montgomery was planning to invade Normandy in the north of France. He wanted the Germans to think he was going to attack the south of France instead. So he sent an actor who looked like him, Meyrick Clifton-James, to North Africa. Meyrick pretended to be Montgomery. German spies said…

THE BRITISH GENERAL IS PLANNING TO ATTACK SOUTHERN FRANCE!

The trick confused the Germans, just as it was supposed to.

### ☙ **DID YOU KNOW…?** ❧

Meyrick Clifton-James lost a finger in the First World War. When he acted as Montgomery he was fitted with a false finger. After the war he acted in a film … about how he acted as General Montgomery. It made him famous.

There was a second Montgomery lookalike called Keith Banwell. He never became famous. He wasn't quite right. He was too tall to play the little general. What did the British do?

**a)** Told him to stand in a hole in the ground when photos were taken.

**b)** Gave him an operation to cut his legs short.

**c)** Told him to stay in the car when he travelled round.

**Answer:**

**c)** Banwell got really fed up with this and asked to go back to fighting as a soldier.

## Batty idea

WHAT A BLAST!

*TIE SMALL FIREBOMBS TO BATS.*
*DROP THE BATS FROM BOMBERS.*
*WHEN THE BATS LAND ON AN ENEMY*
*CITY THEY WILL ROOST.*
*THEN THE BOMBS WILL FLARE AND THE*
*BUILDINGS WILL BURN DOWN.*

This daft idea came from a US dentist, Lytle Adams (who must have had a Lytle brain).

Still President Roosevelt said 'yes' and some tests showed

that the bat bombs worked! They were never used in the war. Only the bats were burned.

## Magical maps

Spies needed maps but would be shot if they were caught with one in their pocket. So maps were cut into 52 pieces and each piece sandwiched into a playing card. When the agent was safely out of sight he or she could peel off the face of the card and put the 52 pieces together to make the map again.

## Corpse checks

Richard Sakakida had Japanese parents and looked Japanese, but was born in America. When America went to war with Japan he was sent to mix with the Japanese people and find out their secrets.

Most Japanese soldiers kept diaries where they wrote about the battle plans – very useful to the American army.

How did Richard get his hands on those diaries?

He went into a battle area when the fighting was over. He searched the blood-soaked uniforms of the Japanese corpses.

Nice job.

# RUTHLESS RESISTANCE

If the enemy took over your country they were said to 'occupy' it. And if you lived in an 'occupied' country you could try to fight back. You became part of a 'Resistance' movement. In France the Resistance was known as the Maquis.

The British SOE went in to help the Resistance wherever they could. They gave them weapons, training and money to carry on the fight.

And Resistance fighters had to be ruthless to survive. The German army occupied the island of Crete. Terrifying stories went around...

IF THE PEOPLE OF CRETE CAPTURE YOU THEY DON'T JUST KILL YOU – THEY CUT UP YOUR BODY INTO LITTLE PIECES!

SOUNDS DICEY!

The Germans soldiers killed many innocent people because they were afraid of the chop. Between May and September 1941 1,135 ordinary Cretans were killed. And they weren't at war.

In places like Croatia Resistance fighters were executed. But the Germans hanged them up in the streets of the towns as a message...

THIS IS WHAT HAPPENS TO RESISTANCE FIGHTERS

## Life lines

If a British airman crashed in France, he wanted to escape back to Britain before the German army locked him up. The Resistance had a way of passing him from one safe house to another till the airman reached the border and escaped. The airman was passed along a 'line'.

If you were caught helping someone to escape you would be executed.

A Belgian woman called Andrée de Jongh ran the Comet Line and helped over 700 airmen to escape. Then SHE was captured and sent to a German concentration camp. She lived.

## Trick trot

In a French village the Germans took over a cottage owned by an old French woman. Their maps and plans were pinned all over the walls but were guarded, even at night.

The old woman sent a message to the local Resistance agent telling him to come with a camera. She gave the German guard coffee full of herbs that gave him diarrhoea.

Every time the guard trotted off to the toilet at the bottom of the garden the agent slipped in and took photos of the maps!

## Life-lie

• Krystyna Skarbek was from Poland. When the Germans invaded she escaped to Britain and joined the SOE. She was sent to help the French Resistance.

After a lot of brave work she was arrested by the Gestapo in August 1944. They decided to shoot her. Krystyna decided the only way out was to try telling a whacking great lie. She asked to meet the Gestapo chief and told him a story...

It worked. Krystyna and her friends went free.

• Another SOE agent who lied her way out of trouble was Eileen Nearne. The Gestapo caught her at her radio, sending secret messages back to Britain. The Gestapo tortured her. She told them she was just a little shop girl who knew nothing. They believed her! But she was sent to Ravensbrück camp anyway. While she was being moved she managed to escape and was rescued by the American army that was marching towards Ravensbrück.

• Odette Sansom (1912–1995) landed near Cassis in November 1942. She worked with SOE fighters and became a messenger to one of them, Peter Churchill (1909–1972). They were arrested by a German who had pretended to be a friend. Odette was tortured and tried to say Peter Churchill was innocent. Finally she told the Germans that (a) Peter was her husband and (b) Brit Prime Minister Winston Churchill was his uncle. The Germans believed her and set her free.

---

### ❧ DID YOU KNOW…? ❧

When the war ended Krystyna Skarbek was out of a job. After six years of dangerous and exhausting work she was given four weeks' wages and left to look after herself.

She lived in poverty. In 1952 she moved into a cheap London hotel. A crazy seaman stabbed her to death.

Krystyna Skarbek survived the Gestapo in wartime – she couldn't survive Britain in peacetime.

---

## Awful assassins

If a French person helped the Germans to conquer their own country, France, they were called 'collaborators'. They would often betray their friends to the German spy-catchers. Every defeated country had its own collaborators.

These collaborators were hated even more than the enemy soldiers and many Resistance workers set out to assassinate them.

### Grande finale

Ivar Grande was a collaborator in Norway and in 1943 the local Resistance set out to kill him. First they plotted to use hand grenades but…

Then they plotted to use an SOE Welrod gun … a small pistol that a spy could take apart and hide. It had a silencer for quiet killing but…

The agents killed him with another special SOE weapon – a machine gun called a Sten gun, fitted with a silencer.

When they shot him Grande was riding his bike home. He ended up wheelie dead.

## ❧ DID YOU KNOW…? ❧

When British students want to raise money they have a week of raising money with stunts, jokes and collections. They call it 'Rag Week'.

In 1943 the SOE decided to have a week of killing Nazis and collaborators in Belgium and France. They made it into a secret joke…

## Bed bug

A German general, Wilhelm Kube, was resting in a Russian town. At midnight he said...

I AM OFF TO BED!

The serving girl smiled and said...

NIGHT NIGHT, SLEEP TIGHT ... MIND THE BOMBS DON'T BITE!

But she was one of the Russian Resistance. The serving girl and her friends slipped out of the hotel. A minute later there was a massive bang. The hotel and the general were scattered over the snowy streets.

The girl had planted a bomb in his bed.

## Smoking gun

The Japanese spies learned tricks from the SOE. They invented a cigarette lighter that was also a one-shot gun. If a spy could get close enough to an enemy it could kill.

Or it could be left for an enemy to find. When they tried to use it to light a cigarette then the bullet would go up their nose.

# SAVAGE SABOTAGE

$S$pies and Resistance fighters didn't just report what the enemy was doing. They also tried to destroy enemy weapons, burn their fuel supplies, wreck their trains, tanks and lorries, and kill their soldiers.

This wrecking is known as 'sabotage'. Here are a few horrible hints.

## 1 Coal holes

Want to blow up a German steam train? Steam locos burn coal. Throw in a few lumps of special secret exploding coal and let the driver blow it up for you!

## 2 Bully boys

The Brits were desperate to stop German tanks being made in the French Citroën factory. They dropped bombs. It didn't work.

So a British spy called Henry Ree went to Mr Citroën and said...

Ree's wreckers blew up machines. When new ones were sent along the canal from Germany the barges were sunk.

After the war ended Henry Ree went back to his old job ... as a teacher.

## 3 Home hints

Another way to sabotage an army is to make the soldiers give in.

The USA used the half-Japanese spy Richard Sakakida to send messages to Japanese soldiers. He rolled the messages into a little 4 cm tube and used a catapult to fire them into the Japanese army camps. They said...

> *It is cherry blossom time back in your home town, and the army have sent you here to the jungles. You should be at home with your families and loved ones smelling the cherry blossom. So why go on with this silly battle? Come and surrender with this leaflet and we will send you back to your home, your family and friends.*

The British air force also used to drop leaflets over German towns telling the Germans to give up because they couldn't win.

## 4 Air today, gone tomorrow

Some people believe spy sabotage began BEFORE the war. There is a mystery about a new British plane that disappeared.

On February 24 1938 a new Brit Wellington bomber set off for a secret test flight. It never returned.

Some believe that the German air force had found out about the flight and shot the plane down near the Scottish coast.

German divers then recovered the wreckage and took it back to Germany on a submarine.

## 5 Twisted teacher

In 1939, before the war, a USA newspaper report said…

A German spy in America wanted to know how it worked. Did he break into the army stores? Did he attack a supply truck?

No. He wrote to the army and said…

DEAR SIR,
I AM A TEACHER AND WANT TO EXPLAIN THE NEW GAS MASK TO MY STUDENTS. CAN YOU SEND ME THE PLANS, PLEASE? OF COURSE I WILL KEEP THEM SECRET.
YPS NAMREGA

What a cheek!
The army said 'yes' and sent the plans.
A week later they were in Germany.

## 6 Thumb-thing nasty

The SOE invented the 'Thumb-knife' for their agents to carry.

This little blade could be hidden in the hand but slip over the thumb to make a small dagger.

Great for cutting enemy phone wires … or enemy throats.

## 7 Something fishy

Hand grenades were sent to Norway for the Resistance fighters to use. They were hidden inside fish cakes.

Be careful how you open them or you may end up with no fishfingers.

## 8 Blow up a train

GO TO THE RAILWAY TRACK. DRIVE A STEEL TUBE INTO THE GROUND SO YOU HAVE A DEEP HOLE...

DROP A SMALL CHARGE INTO THE HOLE AND EXPLODE IT SO YOU HAVE A SMALL CAVE UNDER THE TRACK

FILL THE LITTLE CAVE WITH 20 KILOS OF EXPLOSIVE AND FIT A SWITCH. GET AS FAR AWAY AS YOU CAN

THE SHAKING OF THE TRAIN WILL MAKE THE SWITCH CLOSE AND BANG!

The problem was the switch sometimes went 'Bang' if you shook the ground as you ran away. So Resistance bombers put salt in the switch. Then they added water. The water made the salt dissolve and set the switch. The bombers had time to get away.

## 9 Bath bomb

In Egypt British agents left hotel bathrooms booby-trapped. When the Germans arrived and wanted a bath they pulled out the bath plug ... and set off a bomb.

The trouble was the top generals didn't get the bath ready ... their servants did. It was the servants who died.

## 10 Troop trips

The French Resistance knew where the Germans stored their ammunition. An agent sent a message to London telling them where the store was and the British sent bombers to destroy it.

The Resistance were cunning. When the bombs started to fall the guards fled from the camps to hide in the woods. But the Resistance had laid tripwires that the guards couldn't see in the darkness. They set off bombs that blew them up.

Bombed if they stayed in camp, bombed if they didn't.

# TORTURE
# OF THE TEST

Can you face the torture of the test? If not then find a teacher to torture with these quick questions.

1 SOE spies had a pen that fired a bullet. True/false?

2 The Wel-bum was made at the SOE works at Welwyn (that's true). It was invented to fire bullets out of the back of your trousers if you were being chased. True/false?

3 'Sleeping Beauty' was a top woman spy. True/false?

4 Nasty Nazi Reinhard Heydrich was killed by his car seat. True/false?

5 The British SOE dropped Watercress on a parachute to their spies in Holland. True/false?

6 A French woman had a secret message written on her bottom. True/false?

**7** A British general left secret plans on the bus. True/false?

**8** British spies carried balloons into France (that's true). They needed the balloons so that spies could hold children's parties. True/false?

**9** Germans planted bombs under their own telegraph poles. True/false?

**10** British bombs didn't always work but German traps always did. True/false?

**Answers:**

**1 True.** They also had a smoker's pipe and a cigarette that fired a little bullet. If a spy was stopped and searched the enemy might not spot the weapon. The trouble was the bullets were very small and it was hard to kill an enemy with them.

**2 False.** The Wel-bum was the name given to a little electric motor that pushed a secret swimmer through the water. It stopped him getting tired and left his hands free to plant bombs under ships. But it was useless and sent the swimmers round in circles.

**3 False.** 'Sleeping Beauty' was a spy canoe that could travel underwater if it needed to stay hidden. The inventor made a full-size model. He then climbed into it for a nap. So his friends named his canoe 'Sleeping Beauty'.

**4 True.** Heydrich was attacked by Czech Resistance fighters. A bomb wounded him but he was still able to chase after the Czechs … even though he had no bullets in his gun.

But soon afterwards, Heydrich died from blood poisoning. Bits of dirty car seats had been driven into the bomb wounds. It was the dirt that killed him, not the bomb.

**5 True.** British secret agents in Holland were given the names of vegetables. 'Watercress' was one of them. (Agents in France were given the names of English jobs.)

'Watercress' was really Arnold Baatsen and he was dropped into the waiting arms of the German army. A Dutch spy, Huburtus Lauwens, had been captured and was passing on all SOE messages to the enemy. The Germans used him.

TELL THEM *WATERCRESS* ARRIVED SAFELY. AND TO *PLANT* MORE SPIES! HEH! HEH!

The Brits sent 60 agents to Holland and they were all captured. Most were shot.

But 'Cabbage' escaped back to Britain.

**6 False.** But the woman WAS an agent and the Germans did believe they had found a secret message printed on her bottom.

The woman was 72 years old and known as 'Madame'. She went to the toilet on a hot train trip to Paris. The toilet was disgusting so she spread newspaper on the seat. The print from the paper stuck to her bum.

German spy-catchers were checking everyone ... and everywhere. They were sure they had caught a spy when they saw the print.

They let her go when they worked out what had happened.

**7 True.** In 1944 the officer was given secret plans by Winston Churchill. They were for Operation Torch – an attack on North Africa. He took them home to read them ... but left them on the bus. A woman picked them up and gave them to some soldiers who handed them to the army.

No one knows if they were seen by spies.

The maps for the attack on North Africa were printed and packed on a lorry. On the way back to London the packing broke and the maps of North Africa were scattered over England.

Torch was NOT a very secret secret.

**8 False.** The balloons were given to agents to pull over bombs to keep them dry.

**9 True.** In Greece the German army was fed up with Resistance workers cutting telephone poles. They set up some poles with hidden wires. If a telephone pole was cut a bomb exploded ... and the splinters would be blown into the Resistance worker.

**10 False.** Luckily, German booby traps didn't all work. A Scottish soldier found a cellar full of Scotch whisky. It had been set to explode if anyone took a bottle. The soldier took some bottles back to his friends and there was no explosion. He said...

I CAN'T UNDERSTAND WHY THEY ARE ALL TIED UP WITH BITS OF STRING!

# BOOBY TRAPS

A booby is a stupid bird that lets itself be caught by hand. So a booby trap is a trick to catch an idiot. Schoolchildren have been trying this for years. The drawing pin on the seat or something placed over a half-open door. When the booby walks in the trap falls...

| EXERCISE BOOKS | PLASTIC BUCKET OF COLD WATER | METAL BUCKET OF BOILING OIL |
| NICE TEACHER | NASTY TEACHER | HISTORY TEACHER |

Spies of the Second World War learned to make booby traps and soldiers borrowed their ideas to kill other soldiers.

### Trap doors

The old door trick was used in the Second World War. Some Germans were on the run. They left the house where they had been living but wired the door to a bomb. The British soldiers came along and said...

AH! A NICE PLACE TO SPEND THE NIGHT!

But when they pushed the door they pulled a wire and the wire set off a bomb.

So Brit soldiers learned not to walk into that trap. One group saw an open door…

> THIS TIME WE GO IN THROUGH THE WINDOW…
>
> WE FASTEN OUR OWN WIRE TO THE DOOR
>
> WE HIDE IN THIS NICE DEEP TRENCH ACROSS THE ROAD
>
> THEN WE PULL OUR WIRE AND OPEN THE DOOR…
>
> THE TRENCH WAS BOOBY TRAPPED. THEY WERE ALL KILLED

If you want to be a spy then that's the way to think. Sneaky. But the bad news is booby traps were banned in 1981. You can't use them – even in a war.

**Ooops swoops**
German invaders could land on a British seaside pier and come ashore with dry feet. In 1941 the SOE set booby traps on the piers at Brighton, Worthing and Eastbourne.

At Brighton they laid bombs and set the tripwires. As the SOE set off for home there was a huge explosion.

Were the Germans here already? No. The wire had been tripped by a seagull.

Bits of pier flew everywhere and set off the other tripwires.

The pier was wrecked … and the seagull wasn't too good either.

## Booby books

The SOE invented a mine bomb that looked like a book. Leave it on an enemy desk.

When he opens the book it explodes.

### HORRIBLE HISTORIES WARNING:

Beware! Make sure this is not an exploding book.
Make sure you are wearing a suit of armour and sitting
in a bath before you turn the page!

## Blowing noses

Brit Home Guards built a secret hiding-place in Sussex in case they had to defend the county.

Local people started wandering around to see what was going on. To get rid of the nosey people an SOE worker set booby traps with small explosions.

But one went off as he tried to set it … and damaged his face.

## Losing your bottle

In the battles in North Africa water was precious. Agents for the Italian army scattered water bottles for British soldiers to find.

If you pulled out the cork for a drink, you set off a bomb. Water way to go.

The German agents also left free 'gifts' lying around that contained bombs...

> ❧ A WHISTLE. BLOW IT AND BLOW OUT YOUR BRAINS.
> ❧ AN EXPLODING BAR OF CHOCOLATE
> ❧ PACKETS OF SWEETS FOR A SORE THROAT - INSIDE WERE FIRE BOMBS
> ❧ A PEAR TREE WITH FRUIT THAT EXPLODES WHEN YOU PLUCK IT
> ❧ EXPLODING PIANOS
> ❧ A CHILD'S DOLL - CUDDLY KILLER
> ❧ A PLATE OF FRESH FOOD - BANGERS AND MASH
> ❧ EXPLODING ROWING BOATS
> ❧ CAMERAS THAT BLOW UP IN YOUR FACE WHEN YOU TAKE A PHOTO

## Sweet revenge

Andy Larsen was an SOE agent in Denmark. A friend of the Nazis, Grete Lorte, betrayed him and he was executed.

Andy's friends got some Nobel 808 explosive – which smells like marzipan – and wrapped it like a box of chocolates. They sent it to Grete.

Sadly Grete was not at home when the sweet surprise arrived. Her greedy boyfriend decided to pig into the choccies himself.

He tore it open ... and blew himself to pieces.

## Slicing Samurai

Soldiers like to take home 'prizes' from the wars. In the war against Japan the greatest prize was to take home a real Japanese Samurai sword.

So, of course, the Japanese left Samurai swords behind – booby-trapped.

As soon as you pulled one from the wall a grenade would go off or the handle would explode.

You won the sword – but you lost your hand.

The Japanese also left booby-trapped birds ... dead chickens, hanging from a tree, waiting for hungry soldiers to snatch them.

WHY DON'T YOU TAKE ONE?

TWO CHICKEN!

And you would have been crazy to try and take the wristwatch off the arm of a dead Japanese officer ... it was probably attached to a bomb.

A time bomb? Of course the corpse was blown apart too.

## Well and truly dead

The Japanese also booby-trapped wells so Brit soldiers would die of thirst. But it didn't always work. At Arakan in the Philippines Islands the Brits gave a job to a boy of ten and a girl of five ... to fetch water from the well.

The well was booby-trapped. The boy was blown apart and the girl had an arm blown off and died soon after.

But, most horrible of all, bits of the boy were blown into the well ... so the Brits couldn't drink the water anyway.

# CLEVER CAMOUFLAGE

Camouflage is the trick of making something look like something else. One of the **SOE** experts was a film director before the war. He was good at special effects.

He made…

A LIPSTICK HOLDER TO CARRY MESSAGES

A PAIR OF WOODEN SHOES (CLOGS) THAT HELD EXPLOSIVES

A BOMB IN A WINE BOTTLE

A LARGE FISH THAT HELD A MACHINE GUN

A RADIO IN A VACUUM CLEANER

A BICYCLE PUMP THAT WORKED WITH SHORT STROKES – IT EXPLODED WITH A LONG ONE

SUITCASES THAT HID SPY RADIOS

A RADIO IN A BLOW-UP RUBBER ARMCHAIR

The trick with the bicycle pump was to let down an enemy's bike tyres and leave your pump in place of his.

Some of the SOE's greatest inventions were...

**Deadly droppings**
Bombs were made to look like animal droppings. Enemy cars drove over them and their tyres burst.

But the droppings changed from country to country.

How did the SOE in England find out what African camel droppings looked like?

They looked at London zoo poo!

**Roasting rats**
Rats are everywhere. German workers would find dead ones in factories and throw them on the furnaces.

The SOE made exploding rats. They shoved a stick of explosive up a dead rat's bum. Spies dropped the rats in the factory coal.

The rats exploded inside the boilers and wrecked them.

Soon German workers were scared to throw dead rats on the fire ... even real, harmless dead rats ... so the dead rats lay there and spread disease.

## Plaster parsnips and crafty coconuts

Agents needed to camouflage their secret weapons or hide their messages.

The SOE came up with fruit and vegetables that were hollow and made of painted plaster. In Thailand they made special fruit for the Far East including:

### PINEAPPLES • PAWPAW • MANGOES • COCONUTS

## Fake figures

Statues made from ivory were popular in the Far East. The SOE made their own statues – except they weren't made from ivory, they were carved from TNT explosive.

## Invisible ships

It wasn't only the SOE who tried camouflage tricks, of course.

In 1943, it is said, the Americans were trying an experiment to make their warships invisible. The best camouflage of all! With massive magnets they could 'bend' light so the enemy couldn't see the American warship till it was too late.

Some people believe this was so secret no one will talk about it. The experiment was a success ... and a disaster. It is known as 'The Philadelphia Experiment'.

It is said the ship USS Eldridge had the invisible machine switched on and vanished for four hours. When it appeared again the crew had all gone mad. But one sailor, Edward Cameron, came up with a fantastic story...

I WAS ON USS ELDRIDGE IN 1944. WE VANISHED AND STEPPED OFF THE SHIP IN 1989 – THE INVISIBLE MACHINE IS REALLY A TIME MACHINE!

Hmmm! Do you believe that? Some people do!
A Brit inventor, Lieutenant Donald Currie, said…

SHIPS WILL BE ALMOST INVISIBLE IF YOU PAINT THEM OFF-WHITE

WHAT NONSENSE!

The navy said he was daft but they let him paint a ship, HMS Broke. What happened? A trawler ship crashed into HMS Broke! The trawler captain said…

I DIDN'T SEE IT! IT WAS LIKE IT WAS INVISIBLE!

WELL! BLESS MY SOCKS!

### Can crash
The SOE made bombs in the shape of food tins. Spies were told to leave them in old houses. When soldiers came around they would often take the tins away to eat.

As soon as they tried to open a tin it exploded and turned them into tinned mincemeat.

### Radio-set sneakiness
Spies need their radios as much as anything. In the Second World War they were large and hard to hide.

The SOE came up with all sorts of camouflage so agents could carry radios round the country and look like the locals.

They were hidden in some odd things. Can you spot the things in this pile that were NOT used to hide a spy radio?

10 A RUBBER ARMCHAIR

7 A STUFFED DOG

9 A VACUUM CLEANER

5 A RADIO (A CLEVER ONE THAT!)

8 A RECORD PLAYER

1 AN ARTIST'S PAINT BOX

2 A BUNDLE OF FIREWOOD

3 A PAIR OF BOOTS

4 BATHROOM SCALES

6 A ROCK

**Answer:**
3 and 7 were NOT used but the others were.

The rubber armchair could be pumped up and fitted with seat covers to look like a real chair. The radio was hidden under the seat.

The record player was sent with records – French tunes, of course – and they really played.

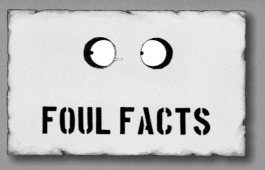

# FOUL FACTS

Weird things happen in wartime. If there were a top ten of disgusting spy facts then this could be it...

## 1 Bright idea

Spies need money. But a lot of cash can get pinched. A Brit spy in Yugoslavia was murdered for the cash he was carrying. Then the SOE came up with the answer...

SEND THE AGENTS IN WITH DIAMONDS. EASIER TO HIDE THAN MONEY

HIDE? WHERE CAN YOU HIDE DIAMONDS IF THE GERMANS SEARCH YOU?

Well? What is the answer? Can you think of the best place? The SOE did...

STICK THEM UP THE AGENT'S BUM!

POO!

And that's what they did. But the plan didn't work too well.
• The Germans started to search in the bums of suspects.
• Some agents went to the loo and lost the diamonds.

In the end they gave up that idea. In a top ten of spy tricks where would that come?

Bottom.

## 2 Well-laid plans

A group of fighters asked for a supply of eggs. So the SOE experts came up with this idea. They...

It worked. Of course you'd need a lot of luck ... the chicken needed a lot of pluck and even more cluck.

Egg-cellent idea?

## 3 A bad case

Not all spy gadgets worked. One spy in Thailand, David Smiley, had a briefcase that could be set to explode if he was attacked. The secret papers would be burned and useless to the enemy. But a spy chief said...

*Poor David took an agent's briefcase with him. Something went wrong with it and it blew up, badly hurting his arm. By the time we got a doctor to him he was picking maggots out of his arm.*

David Smiley said…

*My eyes were so burned, with the skin black and hard, that i couldn't open them again. all the nails were burned off both hands and the flesh was burned to the bone on four fingers of the left hand.*

Over-cooked pies are horrible … over-cooked spies are worse.

## 4 Italian whine

The SOE invented a chemical that was added to wine. The wine still tasted nice so a group of Italian generals drank it the night before a battle.

But the chemicals made the generals run to the toilet all night long for never-ending poos.

The next day the Italians lost the battle.

YOU COULD SAY THEY MET THEIR WATER-LOO!

## 5 Wet wonder

Spies who paddled an underwater canoe wore wet suits. What was the SOE's charming name for this rubber suit?

**a)** The Sticky Life Suit

**b)** The Clammy Death Suit

**c)** The Slippery Black Suit

**Answer:**

**c)** Would YOU like to climb into something called a Death Suit?

## 6 Tasty teeth

The SOE invented a white paste. You could use it to write nasty messages on windows, like 'Hitler smells!' It couldn't be washed off.

The SOE sent the paste off to its North African spies in toothpaste tubes ... but forgot to tell the spies what was REALLY in the tubes.

Some agents tried to clean their teeth and ended up with burned tongues and gums.

## 7 Shooting pains

Sometimes a spy has to kill someone in cold blood. How does it feel?

SOE agent Peggy Taylor (1920–2006) shot and killed a German Gestapo colonel when she was 21. She said simply…

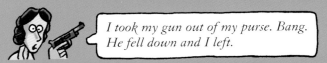

*I took my gun out of my purse. Bang. He fell down and I left.*

## 8 Skull holiday

Elena Rzhevskaya was part of a secret Russian team. She reached Berlin in May 1945 as the Germans surrendered.

Hitler had killed himself ... or had he? The Germans wanted to be quite sure. A Russian soldier had found Hitler's body – the corpse had been burned with petrol to stop the Russians getting their hands on it. Elena went to the grave and watched as a doctor tore off the corpse's jawbone with some flesh still sticking to it.

She popped it into a box lined with satin. She held one of the world's great secrets.

Then the Russian team had to rush through ruined Berlin looking for one man: Hitler's dentist. He had vanished. But they found his assistant who checked the files.

Yes, it was Hitler's jawbone. Yes, the nasty Nazi was dead. Elena took her gruesome box back to Russia.

## 9 Witch way

A British woman, Helen Duncan, said she could talk to spirits of the dead. One day she said she had spoken to a sailor who had been killed when his ship had been sunk. She said the ship was HMS Barham ... and she was right. It had been sunk even though the government was keeping it secret.

The woman was a danger. What other 'secrets' would she give away? How could they stop her?

In March 1944 she was sentenced to nine months in prison under an old law that no one ever used ... the law against witches.

# BLASTING BOMBS

**B**ombs are dangerous ... for the person setting them off! You have to make sure you are well away when the thing explodes. One way of doing this is by using a timer.

### Powerful pencils

Spies often used a 'pencil' timer.

The explosion happened when a spring went ping and drove the striker into the exploding cap.

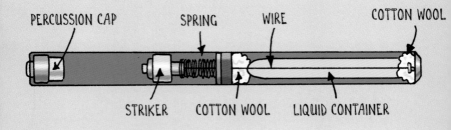

PERCUSSION CAP    SPRING    WIRE    COTTON WOOL

STRIKER    COTTON WOOL    LIQUID CONTAINER

Crush the bubble of liquid till it drips on the wire. The wire burns through and lets the spring go.

Some liquid was strong and set the explosion off in ten minutes. And some liquid was weak and would take a day to go off ... that gives you lots of time to get away!

## ❧ DID YOU KNOW…? ❧

Spies complained that pencil timers could go off after three minutes. Others didn't go off at all. The liquid didn't work very well in the cold. On 13 March 1943 some German soldiers sent a bomb with a pencil timer on to a plane with Adolf Hitler. They watched the plane take off. Nothing happened. They reckoned the aircraft heater wasn't working so the pencil timer was too cold to work.

In 1944 another pencil timer was put in a briefcase full of explosive. The case was left at the feet of Adolf Hitler in a meeting. This time the timer DID work … but someone had moved the case and Hitler just had his trousers blown off.

**Odd but true…**

Why didn't the SOE experts try out their pencil timers to see how they would work in the cold?

Because they didn't have a fridge!

The lives of dozens of spies in cold countries were at risk because the experts didn't have something as common as a fridge. It chills you to think of that.

**Flaming hot**

Not all spy bombs exploded with a bang. Some just glowed into a burst of heat and set fire to enemy buildings. These bombs are called 'incendiaries'.

The flaming liquid could be held in all sorts of secret ways. The SOE tried incendiary…

- cigarettes
- cough mixture
- peanuts … more peanut splutter than peanut butter
- arrows – sort of Robin Red-hot Hood

The Brits were worried that the German spies might send exploding cigars, or poisoned cigars, to Brit Prime Minister Winston Churchill.

So they tested the cigars on mice!

The mice – and Churchill – lived.

## Terrific tactics

A group of SOE agents put bombs under a bridge, to explode when they pressed a button.

But they wanted to kill Germans, not just blow up the bridge.

They scattered tyre-bursters on the road about a hundred metres before the bridge. German lorries ran over them and came to a stop to see what had happened.

They stopped on the bridge. The agents pressed the button. Bridge and enemy went up in the air. Nasty.

# DEAD WRONG

**S**pies made mistakes. Spy mistakes can cost lives.

**1** On 14 May 1941 German spy Karel Richter dropped into England on a parachute. He buried the parachute. Sadly crackpot Karel also buried his food supplies by mistake. After two days he was ill with hunger and the police caught him when he was taken to hospital. He was hanged. At least he didn't die hungry.

**2** Scotland was also a good place to land a German spy. There were miles of deserted coastline where secret agents could be landed without being spotted. In September 1940 three German spies landed in a seaplane near Buckie then rowed ashore in a dinghy. Three bicycles were lowered into the dinghy but dropped into the sea. The spies had expected to cycle 600 miles to London! They set off to catch the train.

As they plodded to the station their shoes were soaked in salt water. A sharp-eyed stationmaster noticed the stains and called the police. The two men were hanged. The woman was spared … because she agreed to work for Britain.

**3** Many spies in the Second World War were given small poison pills. If they were captured then they could crush the pill between their teeth, swallow the poison and die. This would save them from being tortured and betraying their friends.

Several German spies used the poison pills but there's no record of a British spy ever using one.

A German spy called Hermann Goertz was sent to prison in Ireland for his spying. At the end of the war he was set free and ordered to return to Germany. He thought Germany was still run by the Nazis and he'd be shot when he landed, so he took the poison and killed himself.

In fact he would have been perfectly safe.

**4** Many SOE agents landed in France in little Lysander aeroplanes. But they were easier to trace than agents who landed by parachute.

Of the eleven women agents who arrived in France by Lysander aircraft, eight were captured, often within months of landing.

Four came to a cruel end…

• Vera Eugenie Leigh (1903–1944), aged 40, was one of these agents. She became a messenger between Paris and the Yonne river Resistance fighters. She was arrested in 1943.

• 28-year-old Diana Hope Rowden (1915–1944) was a messenger in the Dijon area and was arrested at almost the same time.

• 24-year-old Andrée Raymonde Borrel (1919–1944) was a French shop girl who had worked for the Resistance before being parachuted back in 1942 to be a messenger in Paris.

• The fourth was Sonia Olschanesky (1923–1944), a French-born agent used by the SOE as a messenger in Paris, though she had not been trained by the SOE.

All four were arrested and held in a cell together in Natzweiler camp on 6 July 1944.

That evening they were led, one by one, to the camp crematorium, where they were injected with deadly phenol and their bodies burnt.

**5** The German Gestapo seemed to like executing captured

British women in groups of four.

At Dachau concentration camp they held…

• Yolande Elsa Maria Beekman (1911–1944), who had been a wireless operator, but made the mistake of meeting another agent in a café.

• Noor Inayat Khan (1914–1944), who had been a children's author before the war but became a radio operator for the Resistance. Her mistake was to trust a German agent who betrayed her.

• Elaine Sophie Plewman (1917–1944), who was sent by parachute to act as a messenger in Marseilles, but was betrayed.

• Madeleine Damerment (1917–1944), sent as a messenger, who had the bad luck to be captured by the Germans as soon as her parachute hit the ground.

The four agents spent a night alone in a cell with no windows.

Next morning they were taken to the crematorium yard at Dachau. The yard was covered in sand. The sand helped soak up the blood of the dead – just like in the Roman arenas.

The women knelt down.

They held hands.

They were shot neatly through the back of the head.

**6** Some spies carried a 'sleeve gun': a one-shot pistol that was hidden under your jacket sleeve. It had a safety catch … but it wasn't a very good one. Some agents managed to shoot themselves in the foot!

**7** Some spies were dropped into France with a special little motorbike. It was folded up in a box and dropped on a parachute. It could travel about 90 miles – on good roads.

The trouble was, it was useless on fields and cart tracks. You had to stick to main roads … the roads the German army used!

**8** Alphons Timmerman entered Britain and said he was escaping the Nazis in his home country, Belgium. He was taken in for some questions, but the officer noticed three odd things in his pocket.

- an envelope of white powder
- a bunch of orange sticks
- a piece of cotton wool

Timmerman was arrested, tried and hanged. Why?

Because those three things are what many spies used for invisible writing.

**9** Oswald John Job was born in England but had German parents. He seemed to send a lot of letters to friends in Europe. That was odd but not against the law.

A spy-catcher visited Job in his little flat in London and noticed just one odd thing. Job had a lot of keys.

It was a very small flat. Why did he need so many keys?

The keys were tested. They were used to hide invisible inks and secret codes.

Job was hanged.

He was 59 years old when he was executed – the oldest German spy to die in Britain.

**10** The list of enemy spies executed in Britain is…

| NAME | AGE | EXECUTED | METHOD | PRISON |
|---|---|---|---|---|
| JOSE WALDBERG | 22 | 10 December 1940 | Hanging | Pentonville |
| KARL MEIER | 24 | 10 December 1940 | Hanging | Pentonville |
| CHARLES A. VAN DER KIEBOOM | 26 | 17 December 1940 | Hanging | Pentonville |
| GEORGE JOHNSON ARMSTRONG | 38 | 9 July 1941 | Hanging | Wandsworth |
| WERNER HEINRICH WAELTI | 25 | 6 August 1941 | Hanging | Wandsworth |
| KARL THEO DRUCKE | 35 | 6 August 1941 | Hanging | Wandsworth |
| JOSEF JAKOBS | 43 | 15 August 1941 | Firing Squad | Tower of London |
| KARL RICHARD RICHTER | 29 | 10 December 1941 | Hanging | Wandsworth |
| JOSE ESTELLE KEY | 34 | 7 July 1942 | Hanging | Wandsworth |
| ALPHONS L.E. TIMMERMAN | 37 | 7 July 1942 | Hanging | Wandsworth |
| DUNCAN SCOTT-FORD | 21 | 3 November 1942 | Hanging | Wandsworth |
| JOHANNES MARINUS DRONKERS | 46 | 31 December 1942 | Hanging | Wandsworth |
| FRANCISCUS JOHANNES WINTER | 39 | 26 January 1943 | Hanging | Wandsworth |
| OSWALD JOHN JOB | 59 | 16 March 1944 | Hanging | Pentonville |
| PIERRE RICHARD C. NEUKERMANS | 28 | 23 June 1944 | Hanging | Pentonville |
| JOSEPH JAN VANHOVE | 27 | 12 July 1944 | Hanging | Pentonville |
| THEODORE JOHN WILLIAM SCHURCH | 27 | 4 January 1946 | Hanging | Pentonville |

The list of enemy spies who got away with it is shorter ... because there were none. Some of the captured spies started to spy for Britain instead.

# SOE SCIENCE SECRETS

Brit leader Winston Churchill said the SOE was formed for this purpose...

*I want them to set Europe ablaze!*

The SOE became expert at dropping spies into enemy areas. They would report German troops, uncover secrets and destroy whatever helped the enemy – railways, roads, telephones and so on.

They had their own inventors to help them make secret war.

**Tasty tablets**
SOE agents were sent over to France with a kit. They also had tablets A, B, E, K and L. Make sure you get them right!

A CALMS YOU AND STOPS YOU BEING AIR SICK

B PEPS YOU UP AND KEEPS YOU AWAKE

E KNOCKOUT DROPS TO SEND AN ENEMY TO SLEEP

K A SLOW-ACTING SLEEPING PILL TO SEND SOMEONE TO SLEEP FOR FOUR HOURS

L CYANIDE POISON. SUCK IT AND DIE IN 30 SECONDS

Why would you want to kill yourself? It may be better than being tortured by the Gestapo and giving away your friends.

---

**❦ DID YOU KNOW…? ❦**

Your poison 'L' tablet could be hidden in your mouth and would only kill you if you crunched it. It had three thick coatings to stop it leaking by accident.

How did you know if the coating was damaged?

The SOE made the tablets so that your pee would turn blue if your tablet was damaged. By then it would probably be too late.

You could say this idea was a widdle bit dangerous.

---

## SOE special tricks

**1** British pigeons were dropped on miniature parachutes to agents in France. The agents made their reports and the pigeons took them back to Britain. German soldiers soon learned about this and had orders to shoot any suspicious-looking pigeons. The heroic pigeons that did get home safely were often eaten once their messages had been read! Sometimes the spies were lost and starving and ate their feathered friends before they had even flown.

**2** The SOE invented 'nitrated' paper for secrets. Put a match to a sheet of nitrate paper and it vanishes in a flash with hardly any ash. BUT … if you pack a few sheets together and light them, they explode more like a bomb! Still it would make a good excuse for homework…

PLEASE, SIR, THE DOG ATE MY HOMEWORK

**3** Saboteurs got to the crew of a German submarine (or U-boat). They added the scratchy seeds of the Mucuna plant to the soldiers' talcum powder and scattered them in their shirts, underpants or bedclothes. What happened? They itched and itched and itched till their skin was raw and bleeding. The U-boat had to turn back to port because the sailors were driven wild with itchy skin!

**4** The SOE invented tiny glass balls filled with nasty liquid that would make a horrible smell when they were dropped. Yes, the SOE invented the 'stink bomb' and they are still useful for driving the enemy (teachers) mad today!

**5** If you wanted to walk around in an enemy country you needed papers to say who you were. The enemy would give you them and stamp them with ink. You couldn't have papers saying...

So you needed false papers with false stamps. What would you use to make a false stamp?

**a)** a hard-boiled egg

**b)** a cow's nose

**c)** a potato

**Answer:**
**a)** or **c)** were both used. But not a cow's nose – everybody knows a cow's nose smells.

# TORTURE AND TERROR

If you are a soldier and you are taken prisoner you are sent to a prisoner-of-war camp and are supposed to be treated quite well.

But if you are a spy and you are taken prisoner you can be tortured to give up your secrets, executed if you don't ... and probably executed if you do!

If YOU were a spy-catcher, and you HAD to get an enemy spy to talk, could YOU try these terrible tortures?

## Lulu (1915–2007)

Lucie Chevalier was 15 years old when she joined the secret fight against the Germans in her country, Belgium.

Her code-name was Lulu. This teenager…

- spied on German troops
- blew up bridges and a station
- helped to hide escaping British airmen

Towards the end of the war Lucie was captured by Hitler's secret police, the Gestapo. She refused to talk so they tortured her.

WE WILL STRAP YOUR WRISTS TO THE ARMS OF A CHAIR...

WE WILL PULL OUT YOUR FINGERNAILS. WANT TO TALK?

NO!

The Gestapo pretended to execute her three times. Still she didn't give away any secrets.

Lucie was sent to Germany as a slave worker in a gun factory. She escaped even though she was shot in the arm.

By the time she got back to Belgium she was starved and so ill her teeth fell out.

After the war she married and settled in Bridport, Dorset, where she died aged 82.

### Elizabeth Choy (1910–2006)

Elizabeth worked as a canteen helper at a Singapore hospital. The Japanese invaded and many Brits were prisoners in the hospital.

Elizabeth secretly brought food, medicine, money, messages and even radios to British. Then six Japanese ships were sunk in the harbour. The Japanese looked for someone to blame.

She was punished with 200 days of a starvation diet and repeated torture. After the war she wrote…

*I was put into a cell just 4 m by 5 m. There were more than 20 people crammed inside. We knelt from morning till night. Some of us suffered serious sores on our knees.*

*I was the only woman in there. Inside the cell was a tap and underneath it, a hole meant for a toilet. We went to the toilet in full view of everyone. The stink coming from our sweat and toilet waste was suffocating.*

*Our captors beat us up and pumped us up with water as part of the questioning. The feeling of having one's belly pumped full of water and then seeing the water gushing out of the body was hardly bearable.*

*When I refused to talk they … applied electric currents to me.*

*I was held in the centre for more than 200 days. I wore the same clothes for that period of time. Getting a shower was a dream; we felt very lucky to have a little water to wash our faces.*

After 200 days her torturers believed her. Elizabeth survived – 15 other prisoners died from the torture.

How did she feel when she was released? Elizabeth said she forgave the men who tortured her. It was only the war that made them do it.

Still, eight of her torturers were hanged after the war ended.

### Pierre Brossolette (1903–1944)

Pierre Brossolette had fought in the French army until it was defeated. He then started to set up Resistance groups.

Pierre opened a bookshop in Paris where rebels could meet and messages could be passed on.

He escaped capture many times but in 1944 he was shipwrecked as he tried to escape to England. The Gestapo captured him.

He was tortured. Pierre was afraid he would betray his old friends.

He went to the toilet, five floors up, opened the window and threw himself out. He was taken to hospital but died.

Torture or death? Which would you choose?

### Forest Frederick Yeo-Thomas (1901–1964)

Torture didn't always kill you there and then.

Forest Yeo-Thomas went to France to work with Pierre Brossolette. He escaped capture with a clever plan…

**1.** Forest placed his secrets in a coffin.

**2.** He climbed into the coffin with his machine gun and was covered in flowers.

**3.** If the Gestapo searched the funeral car he'd have shot his way out of trouble. They didn't.

**4.** Instead he was taken to a landing strip and flown home in a Lysander aeroplane.

After a coffin escape you would give up and get a safe job back in Britain, wouldn't you?

But when Forest heard his friend had been captured he went back to France to rescue him. A traitor in the Resistance told the Germans where to catch him.

Forest was captured and tortured horribly. The torture didn't kill him at the time – but he was left so weak he died less than 20 years later after a long illness.

### Adrian

The SOE used a Polish spy to report on the Germans in 1944. His code name was 'Adrian'.

As Adrian passed a German airfield he made a sketch on notepaper. Soon afterwards he was arrested but managed to swallow the sketch.

The Gestapo took him to their prison. They…
- searched his clothes
- cut his shoes to pieces
- gave him medicine to make him poo, then checked the poo

They found nothing.

So they tortured him and 'rolled' him between large rubber rollers.

This made him sick. When the Gestapo looked at his sick they found the sketch. He was sent to be executed.

But this story has a happy ending!

An American bombing raid blew the prison doors wide open. Adrian and the other prisoners escaped.

# SPY ENDS

Spies did not live safe and easy lives. Some had miserable lives ... and worse deaths.

## 1 Cicero (real name: Elias Basna)

A German spy, code-named Cicero, sent British secrets from Turkey. The Brits were after him so Cicero had to make a quick getaway. The Germans helped him by giving him £300,000 of British money.

The trouble was the banknotes were all fake. Cicero was arrested and thrown in a Turkish jail – not for spying but for forging money.

### ☠ DID YOU KNOW...? ☠

Germany wanted to print £100 million of fake notes and scatter them round Britain to ruin British banks. Some money WAS given to spies like Cicero. But most of it was dumped, after the war, in a deep lake in Austria.

The head German forger was Bernard Kruger. His plot to ruin British banks didn't work. But Bernard had a second, secret plot that DID work. Bernard used Jewish workers in concentration camps to help him. While they worked for him they were safe from being executed with poison gas in the camps.

Bernard saved many lives.

### 2 King Kong

A German spy in Holland used to be a wrestler so his code name was King Kong. This spy made a monkey out of the British by pretending to work for them.

He was arrested and thrown in jail. He killed himself in prison.

### 3 Sandor Rado

Sandor Rado was a spy for Russia. He told the Russian leader, Stalin, exactly how the Germans were planning to attack them. The Germans were defeated.

Hero Rado? His spy group were arrested. After the war he was tracked down and forced to go back to Russia. Did they give him a medal?

No. Stalin blamed Rado for the spy ring being arrested. Rado was sent to a labour camp for ten years – hard, cold work and food worse than school dinners.

He was released in 1955. He became a teacher. Poor man.

## 4 Admiral Wilhelm Canaris

Admiral Canaris was head of the Nazi navy, but he hated Adolf Hitler. He wanted peace, so he started passing on German secrets to Britain. He was never caught, but he did come to a nasty end.

A group of Hitler's officers plotted to blow up Hitler with a bomb in July 1944. Canaris was one of the group. Four German officers died. What happened to Hitler? All that happened was the bomb blew off his trousers and set fire to his hair.

Canaris was arrested and in April 1945 he was executed – slowly strangled with piano wire. Hitler made a film of the dreadful death and showed it to his generals.

### ❧ DID YOU KNOW...? ❧

The bomb used to try to kill Hitler was made from British SOE explosives. The Germans had captured them and found they were better than German explosives. The SOE weapon-makers would have been pleased!

## 5 Marianne von Mollendorf

Eric Erikson ran an oil company in Sweden and pretended to be a friend of Germany. He told the British where all the German oil factories were and the British were able to bomb them.

Eric used young Marianne von Mollendorf to help him and they fell in love. In 1944 the Nazis took him to a cruel jail called Moabat. But he wasn't going to be executed. He was given a special treat ... he was going to watch spies being shot with machine guns.

He watched as his Marianne was executed.

## 6 Beheaded Brits

Twenty-three British men went to Singapore in October 1944.

The port was used by the enemy Japanese navy. They paddled canoes into the harbour and sank Japanese ships using mines.

Ten were captured. The Japanese later cut off their heads and stuck the heads on poles in Singapore. Two more of the men chewed on poison pills and killed themselves so they would not be captured.

In time the other 11 died fighting.

### 7 US spy shock

When the USA joined the war there were several German spies in the country. Hitler ordered that his spies there should wreck canals and railways, power stations and water supplies.

Eight were caught and were executed in the electric chair. Shocking.

### 8 Dropping Schiller

A German spy was captured and he promised to work for the SOE. The SOE plan was to drop him into Germany with lots of spy stuff and contacts with the German Resistance – a bit like the French Resistance but in Germany.

The spy, code-named Schiller, was dropped into Germany. If he were captured he'd betray his new Brit friends, wouldn't he?

So what did the SOE do? Gave him a parachute that didn't work.

The Germans found the German Resistance 'secrets' … and panicked.

## 9 The Red Orchestra

The Gestapo called Russian spies 'The Red Orchestra'.

The Russian spies were helping Hitler's enemies in Germany.

A group of German traitors were arrested by the Gestapo. Hitler gave the order…

So the Gestapo fastened some butchers' meat hooks to the prison ceiling and hanged the traitors from them.

Gallows let the victim drop and break their neck – they died quickly. The meat-hook method meant the victim was strangled and died slowly.

The meat-hook method was the Gestapo way of executing traitors till the end of the war.

# EPILOGUE

You land in an enemy country. You attack the enemy and help the local people to wreck the factories and railways. You risk being betrayed and beaten, tortured and twisted.

Every day is an awesome adventure.

Exciting?

No. Because an evil enemy will crush everyone who stands in their way as they search for you.

One of the cruellest Nazis was Reinhard Heydrich. Resistance fighters killed him. One Nazi died. But the price the people paid was terrible.

## Czechoslovakia Today

1 June 1942

# MASSACRE AT LIDICE

Hitler's hangman, Reinhard Heydrich, was killed by a freedom fighter's bomb in the Czech capital, Prague, two weeks ago. Yesterday the German SS (top Nazi military organization) exacted their revenge.

They rounded up most of the 450 people in Lidice and shot 172 men. Seven women were shot while trying to escape and the rest were transported to Ravensbrück concentration camp. The 90 children were given new names and sent to Germany to be raised as Germans.

Today the SS will dynamite the town and the rubble will be levelled till not a trace remains.

It may look as if the women and children got off lightly, though 52 died at Ravensbrück – seven of them exterminated by poison gas.

But exactly two years later, the women in a French village were not so lucky…

**French Underground News** 10 JUNE 1944

# TERROR ATTACK AT ORADOUR-SUR-GLANE

**N**azis may call their actions at the little village of Oradour 'revenge' – the rest of the world will call it bloody murder. The German forces massacred everyone they could find in the town and some 642 people were killed.

The Nazis marched into the town demanding to see identity papers and search for explosives. The recent capture of an SS officer by the French Resistance fighters in the region had infuriated the Germans. Witnesses say the Germans herded the men into the barns and barred the women and children in the church.

Then the killings began. The 190 men were shot first and then smoke was seen rising from the farmhouses as the SS bullies burned them. Finally the church was set on fire; women who tried to escape were machine-gunned through the church windows and the grenades that were thrown into the screaming masses killed many more. In all 207 women and children died.

Somehow ten lucky people survived by pretending to be dead till the SS left.

The abandoned village has been left in ruins as a memorial to the victims.

But, most horrible of all, the Nazis had wiped out the wrong village. The German officer had been killed in Oradour-sur-Vayres, south of Limoges. The avengers killed the people of Oradour-sur-Glane, to the north of Limoges.

Spies of the Second World War were brave people and many led exciting lives. Others faced dreadful deaths and brought cruel killing to helpless people.

Spying isn't all cool codes, groovy gadgets and fantastic fun.

# INTERESTING INDEX

Hang on! This isn't one of your boring old indexes. This is a horrible index. It's the only index in the world where you will find camouflaged coconuts, crafty corpses, fake feet and all the other things you really HAVE to know if you want to be a horrible historian. Read it and creep.

assassins, awful 43
Aunt Minnies (secret pictures) 20

balloons 52, 54
banks 86
bats 38–9
batteries, bicycle-driven 32
blood 21, 39, 53, 68, 75
body-snatchers 37
bombs, blasting 6, 21, 31–2, 36, 38–9, 45, 47, 50, 52–6, 58–60, 63, 70–2, 79, 88, 91
booby traps 54–9
books, baffling 27, 30, 57
bottoms 51, 53, 61, 65–6
Brossolette, Pierre (French spy) 22, 84

camels 5–6, 61
camouflage, cunning 60–4
card tricks 27, 39
cheek pads, cheeky 19
cherry blossom, smelling 47
chickens 66
Churchill, Winston (British leader) 43, 54, 72, 78

coconuts, camouflaged 62
codes, cracking 24–8, 76, 93
coffins 36, 84–5
collaborators, 43
corpses, crafty 36–7, 39, 59, 68
creams, coloured 18

D-Day, dire 8, 10
deserts, desperate 5
diarrhoea (runny poo) 41
disguises, disgusting 6, 18–23
dogs 33
donkeys 61
droppings, deadly 61
drops, dead 35

Enigma (German code machine) 24
executions, excruciating 40–2, 58, 76–7, 81–2, 85, 87–90

faces, funny 19–20
factories, foul 36, 46–7, 61, 82, 88, 91
feet, fake 18–19
films, famous 11, 13, 38

**firebombs, ferocious** 36, 38, 58
**First World War, frightful** 38
**fish cakes, fishy** 49

**gadgets, groovy** 29–33, 93
**gas masks, ghastly** 48
**Gestapo** (Nazi secret police) 8, 41–3, 68, 74, 79, 81–2, 84–5, 90
**gifts, gross** 58
**graveyards, grisly** 35

**hair, horrific** 22
**hand grenades, handy** 32, 43–4, 49
**Heydrich, Reinhard** (Nazi nasty) 7, 32, 51, 53, 91
**Hitler, Adolf** (Nazi leader) 7–8, 37, 68–9, 71, 81, 88–90
**horses** 61

**inks, invisible** 34, 76
**itches, irritating** 80

**kit, clever** 22–3
**knickers** 21

**maggots** 66
**maps, magical** 39, 41
**Maquis** (French resistance) 40
**massacres, murderous** 91–2
**mice** 72
**microphones, marvellous** 29
**money, fake** 86–7

**Montgomery, Bernard** (British general) 37–8, 42

**Navahos** (Native Americans) 25–6
**Nazis, nasty** 7–8, 13, 21, 28, 32, 44, 58, 74, 76, 91–3

**oilcans, exploding** 33

**pants** 21, 80
**papers, false** 80
**parachutes, perfect** 30–1, 36, 51, 73–6, 79, 89
**parsnips, plaster** 62
**pee** 79
**pencils, powerful** 70–1
**pens, painful** 33
**Philadelphia Experiment** 62
**piers, perilous** 56–7
**pigeons** 79
**pills, killing** 73–4, 78–9, 89
**poison, putrid** 32, 37, 72–4, 78, 89, 92
**poo** 5–6, 21, 67, 85
**prunes** 29–30

**radios, really useful** 16, 24, 32, 42, 60, 63–4, 75, 83, 90
**Rat Week** 8, 44
**Reed Orchestra** (Russian spies) 90
**Resistance** (freedom fighters) 8, 12, 16–17, 26, 40–6, 49–50, 53–4, 74–5, 84–5, 89–92
**Roosevelt, Franklin** (American president) 39

safe houses 41

Sakakida, Richard (American spy) 39, 47

Samurai swords, sensational 59

sandals, sneaky 18–19

science, secret 78–80

seagulls 56–7

Second World War, scary 6–7, 9, 18, 20, 29, 34, 55, 63, 73, 93

shaving brushes, sizzling 33

ships, invisible 62–3

slaves, suffering 36, 82

Sleeping Beauty 51–2

Sleeve guns 75

Smiley, David (British spy) 66–7

soap, savage 33

Special Operations Executive (SOE) 7–8, 16, 18, 21, 29–33, 36–7, 40–5, 49, 51, 53, 56–8, 60–3, 65–8, 71–2, 74, 78–80, 85, 88–9

Stalin, Joseph (Russian leader) 87

statues, explosive 62

stink bombs 15, 80

tanks, no thanks 5, 46

tear gas 33

thumb-knives, throat-cutting 49

timeline, terrific 7–8

tins, exploding 63

toilets 53, 67, 83–4

torture, terrible 13, 17, 22, 42–3, 51–4, 73, 79, 81–5, 91

trains, wrecking 46, 49

trap doors 55–6

U-boats (German submarines) 80

washing lines, wacky 24

Wel-bum 51–2

White Rose (German freedom fighters) 8

wine, wicked 67

witches 69

writing, invisible 76